Italian Motorcycles

Italian Motorcycles

Classic sports bikes

TIM PARKER

Osprey Colour Series

Published in 1984 by Osprey Publishing Limited,
12–14 Long Acre, London WC2E 9LP
Member company of the George Philip Group

British Library Cataloguing in Publication Data

Parker, Tim
    Italian motorcycles.—(Osprey colour series)
    1. Motorcycles, Italian
    I. Title
    629.2'275'0945   TL440
ISBN 0-85045-576-6

Editor Alan Cathcart
Design Roger Daniels

Filmset by Tameside Filmsetting Limited,
Ashton-under-Lyne, Lancashire
Printed in Hong Kong

Front cover photograph John Lee of Verghera
Engineering near Sudbury, Suffolk built and now
looks after this late 1977 832 Monza MV Agusta.
It's very special with its 861 barrels, Magni
camshaft, 30 mm carbs, exhaust and a multitude of
'home made' parts. The Veglia Borletti rev
counter starts at 5000 rpm

Back cover The Ducati that everyone moans about
– it's neither a 900SS nor a soft GTS, not a 'real'
Ducati, they say. Nonsense; this 1983 900S2,
electric start Desmo, with 600 Pantah-style fairing
is of course a compromise, but one that works.
Shot in Chichester, West Sussex

Half title 1983 Moto Guzzi Le Mans Mark III shot
at Jim Wood's shop in Glendale, California. Some
prefer the earlier round barrel cylinders, but these
will do fine. Still a most desirable bike

Title Laverda's LZ125 range shot from inside the
factory's showroom out through the window to
show the start of the Dolomite foothills looking
north-east. That's where they road test them all

Opposite Italian motorcycles don't come much
more interesting than this Italjet 350 Roadmaster,
seen here at the 1983 Milan show – single cylinder
two-stroke, 6 speed, electric start, liquid cooled,
and handsome. Fast too

Page 6 Historic racing in Italy, at Misano – the
best meeting of its type in the world?

Contents

Introduction

There's no question in my mind that there exists a worldwide following for Italian motorcycles, as opposed to those made in Japan, Germany, even Great Britain. I believe, also, that that enthusiasm has been apparent for many years and is not just a further counter-reaction to the Japanese as a result of the demise of the mainstream British industry. If you have bought this book then you believe this too, or at least you are curious. Above all I hope that the photographs within show off the charisma of the subject.

ITALIAN MOTORCYCLES confines itself to modern Italian sports bikes in the main – most are over 500 cc too – but included are other interesting machines of either the touring or road racing variety where I have felt extra colour is desirable. Off road competition bikes are mostly excluded. You will notice from the credits that the photographs have been taken in several different countries, including Italy, and were taken over a number of years. May I re-iterate my thanks for those who have helped?

In one statement it is possible to summarise what's special about Italian motorcycles, 'when the British were painting nearly all their bikes black (albeit, perhaps, with gold coachlines), the Italians were painting theirs red'. Before I was old enough to know the difference, I guess I just liked the red ones best. My active involvement started in 1974 when I bought a near new Laverda 750SF2 – I was sold on their excellent brochure of the day! I have had a string of Laverdas since and am still fortunate to own a 1975 750SFC (as well as a 1960 50 cc Mini-scooter and a 1962 Bultaco 125TSS). Further fortune has enabled me to ride most big Italian bikes imported to England as well as their Japanese, German, American and British competition. I'm not just a 'Laverda man'.

For no real reason the photographs have been grouped by manufacturer, in alphabetical order, with a final section of 'others'. Italy still has six 'big' bike companies extant at the time of writing – including 'new boy' Cagiva – and one about to disappear – Ducati. Added to the six is MV Agusta and Bimota. The former needs no justification for the four cylinder road bikes from Verghera are the very embodiment of all that 'Italian red' means.

The latter, in spite of their Japanese-sourced engines, are so fine and revered that no book on this subject can afford to be without them.

Enjoy these pages of lovely sports bikes from these most famous of names, *Motos* Benelli, Bimota, Cagiva, Ducati, Guzzi, Laverda, Morini and MV – from Aermacchi, Gilera, Paton *et al*.

Many people have helped – you have my grateful thanks. Three people encouraged me – Alan Cathcart, Andrew Morland and Chloe Parker. The following put up with me. In Italy: Massimo and Piero Laverda at Breganze, plus Fulvio Menegotto; Franco Valentini and Nadia Pavignani at Ducati Meccanica in Bologna; the staff at Bimota in Rimini; the organizers of both the 'historic' meeting at Misano and the Milan motorcycle show. In England: Richard Slater of Slater Bros (Motorcycles) at Collington; Keith Davies, UK's Laverda importer and proprietor of Three Cross Motorcycles near Wimborne, Dorset; Gareth Jones of Cropredy Superbike, Banbury; Roger Winterburn of Windy Corner in Leicester; Phil Todd of Motodd in Croydon; Alan Bell of Miura Engineering in Hayes; Dudley Martin of Speedscene in Huddersfield; John Lee of Verghera Engineering near Sudbury, Suffolk and many others. In the USA: Lance Weil of Rickey Racer in Costa Mesa, California; Steve Carroll of European Cycle Specialties just down the road in Garden Grove; Jim Woods of Woods Motor Shop a little further away in Glendale, as well as Rich McCormack and Gerald Foster. In West Germany: Uwe Witt of Moto Witt, Germany's Laverda importer, in Cologne.

Finally, with the help of Minolta and Kodachrome, it's all my own work. . . .

Tim Parker,
April 1984

Traditionally in books within the Osprey Colour Series the author/photographer is allowed one shot of himself usually in this position in the book. The modesty of the photographers has often meant that they have shown only a reflection of themselves or even hidden themselves in the text asking the reader to guess where. Mike Key in his recent book *LEAD SLEDS* (published in this series in early 1984) showed a picture of his 1940 Chevrolet four door sedan which he had chopped and built himself. In that vein I'm showing my 750SFC Laverda which I have *re*-built twice!

This machine dates from 1975 – confirmed by its wire spoke wheels and magnesium primary side cover with the small electronic ignition 'bump' at its leading edge. The SFC is a marvellous motorcycle. Not only does it look right but it goes well too. In its heyday, say 1972, it was virtually unbeatable in endurance racing – now, in the right hands, on the right day, it'll stay with anything cross-country. Heaven sent.

1 Pesaro
— *the brothers and de Tomaso*
— Benelli

Above and right Since the company was taken over and absorbed into the de Tomaso empire in the 1970s, the company has steadily grown in strength, particularly in Italy, although their actual success is somewhat obscured because of the empire's structure – Moto Guzzi, Innocenti, Maserati and more. Even today, small Benelli two-stroke twins clean up the TT3 racing class in Italy, and these are road bike based.

The whole world heard again from Benelli when their six-cylinder Honda 500 Four-based roadster, as a 750, hit the streets. This is the later 900 Sei with stylish 'group' bodywork. The factory quote 80 horsepower at 8400 rpm

Left and below Behind the brake pedal is the gearbox of the 900 Sei, the one weak link, or was it the clutch too? Reliability wasn't its *forté* inspite of the duplex rear drive chain, a feature more for show than effect. The quality of build didn't match Honda's and the bike hasn't sold as well as hoped

Left 'I remember when . . .'. From any angle the 900 Sei is good looking and that style is matched by good handling, steering and road holding and adequate if not stunning speed. However, although it was the first of the six-cylinders, it couldn't match the pace of Honda's CBX nor the bulk of Kawasaki's Z1300. Perhaps a saving grace is that neither the CBX nor Z1300 has sold to expectation and maybe the world doesn't want six-cylinder road motorcycles at all. If that's the case, then its place in history is that of 'first'. Good examples are worth collecting for this reason alone.

In the window behind is a Guzzi V50 Monza another de Tomaso fledgling to fill the market gap under the big Guzzi vee-twins. Barry Sheene just wants to pass

Below Outside the Classic Bike Show at Belle Vue, Manchester in 1983 was this well-kept 750 Sei. The strange two-tone tank looks out of place although that's how they came and . . .

Above . . . inside the show as a concours entry was this modified 750 Sei which looks hardly used at all. The bikini fairing and the hump seat both give an impression of speed although too much of it will ground the bike too early in corners, especially with the six-into-six exhausts. Benelli six noise is lovely no matter what

Right In the 1960s Benelli produced a series of road racing fours with some success – de Tomaso wanted history to repeat itself, and gain brand loyalty, so he produced this radically styled 250 Quattro in the late '70s. It's a little toy of some character – but few were sold

Overleaf Some would say a real Benelli from the Pesaro brothers – a 1938 4TNE, 500 twin, at Misano – curious 'deformable parallelogram' swinging arm rear suspension

2 Rimini — *BIanchi, MOrri e TAmburini* — Bimota

The Isle of Man in TT week shows up most exotica. Here's an SB2 Bimota hiding a late MV Agusta. Both have suede seats. Note the Suzuki 750 powered SB2's long swingarm which pivots coaxially with the gearbox sprocket for constant rear drive chain tension. The body styling was Bimota at its best (read most adventurous)

Left and below The 750 Suzuki four cylinder powered SB2 grew into the SB3 with their 1000 engine. Bimota, with Massimo Tamburini designing the chassis, grew substantially with this machine. The whole world instantly recognised these bikes for what they were – the most highly prized, handbuilt roadsters in existence. From this point on, almost overnight, the Bimota was the benchmark by which all fine handling bikes were judged. Note the number plate

The Milan motorcycle show, late every two years, is an exciting event at which most Italian manufacturers are proud to exhibit what they are best at. In 1983, the Bimota stand was outstanding – it was always crowded, even at the press only showing. There was the standard range of bikes using Suzuki, Honda and Kawasaki engines and a couple of truely stunning exhibits. Here's one of them.

The bike is the company's SB4 model with Suzuki 1100 four cylinder engine, with special paint. The SB4 has a different style of chassis from the previous SB2 and SB3 – it aligns itself with the HB2 and 3 frames (Honda) in that it has lost the long pivoted swingarm with constant chain tension for a more conventional method, plus paired alloy lower frame cradles milled from solid pieces of Avional which are jig-glued to the fabricated steel tubular chassis. No longer does the frame 'split' in the middle. The wheels are still Campagnolo's cast magnesium, Brembo Goldline brake equipment with full floating discs and new style Forcelli Italia front forks. Michelin radial tyres complement the whole package.

The paint comes from the brush of Aldo Drudi. This design hit the magazine covers with a vengeance, and rightly so. Bimota's demonstrator, the girl with the blonde hair, shows off their new rider/designer wear, offered for the first time at the show to those wealthy enough to buy, or pose

Left It's not often one sees a Bimota in the shop window of a greengrocer, in north-east London. This new KB2 sat there for some weeks although its keeper, Mike Byrne of Newton Equipment, suggested his friendly greengrocer's window, inspite of its stickers, was most suitable.
Those with much experience of Bimotas suggest the 550 Kawasaki powered KB2 Laser is the one to have

Above Back to the Milan show with this SB4 1100 in stock trim. This one shows off Bimota's own composite wheels *à la* Astralite and all that's latest in tyres, brakes and front forks. The Avional lower frame member is clearly visible now. What's also quite evident is the quality of the whole, with each single fitting being executed in the best possible material to the highest standard

Left The latest Bimota KB2 Laser TT showing detail changes in the fairing and tank unit (see the greengrocer's KB2 on the previous page). The chassis for this smaller machine does have the radical engineering of the larger bikes, with its effective coaxial rear suspension with a rising rate rocker-arm

Above Young and old, rich or poor, everyone admires the 'no compromise' Bimota, which vies for the best made, best handling, fastest and most expensive motorcycle in the world

25

Above In late 1983 Tamburini left Bimota to work
with Roberto Gallina in designing a road racing
chassis for HB-Suzuki. Bimota were able to show
their continuing expertise at Milan in 1983
without him – this Honda powered *Tesi* (thesis)
was the star of the show, and a gaze at the future

Right Unashamedly a copy, the HRD Silver Horse
shows what a Bimota 125 might look like. High
quality, high price too, for those in need

3 Varese
— Aermacchi, then Harley-Davidson — Cagiva

Above Master Norton Manx tuner, the late Francis Beart, tried his hand at making Aermacchi singles go fast once the Manx had had its day. He succeeded. His immaculate preparation, rather than radical modification, paid him dividends. Note the familiar Ford green paint. Behind the 350 Aermacchi is a 500 Linto twin — in concept, two 250 Aermacchis side by side. Both are highly prized today

Left Also shot in the Isle of Man during TT week in 1982 was this German registered Aermacchi Harley-Davidson in pretty standard sports trim. The road racers were based on this model

29

Right and below Just superb. This immaculate road
racing Aermacchi Harley-Davidson 350 was on
show before the regularity parades at Misano,
south of Rimini in Italy during the 'Historic GP' in
1982. The detailing is just splendid, from the pile
of the suede seat, to the careful colour matching of
the elastic cords which secure the tank and fairing,
the locking wire and the precise positioning of the
rev counter so that the needle is in the rider's line
of vision when 'on song'.
The close-up of the tank badge reveals the union
between Italian engineering and American money.
It has happened many times in the past and will
happen again – it's difficult to think of a better
case for this co-operation than the horizontal
Aermacchi single

Above and left In 1983 Cagiva, that with the
elephant on the tank, was described as Italy's most
prolific motorcycle manufacturer. Out of the
'ashes' of Aermacchi Harley-Davidson rose the
elephant, and mostly on the back of this type of
two-stroke dual-purpose bike (above in an English
showroom in Yorkshire). If in a few years this has
happened with most sales being confined to Italy,
what happens when they export four-strokes?
The Cagiva poster had yet to be erected – it
hadn't fallen! (Milan, 1983)

Cagiva 350 Ala Azzurra on show for the first time
to buying public, all of whom are still not quite
sure how a Ducati Pantah engine should find its
way into Cagiva's factory in Varese, in northern
Italy. And why it doesn't stay in a Ducati chassis
made in Bologna. Nevertheless, the Cagiva Pantah
is a handsome bike and a good start for them in
breaking into the sports roadster market in 1984.
For the moment the Verlicchi-made frame is
identical to the 'old' Ducati Pantah's as are most of
the mechanicals – the styling is all their own

Another version of the same bike uses the 600 cc
Pantah engine, and this is the one which the rest
of the world is waiting for. The 750 version is on
its way.

The Italian home market is large for 350 cc
engined motorcycles because of their 'value added
tax' thresholds – 125 cc and below is very cheap,
125 to 350 cc affordable, over 350 cc expensive. . . .
Already many road racing Ducati Pantahs have
overnight become Cagiva Pantahs, just with paint
on the tank. The small Ducati vee-twin is in good
hands. See over

Below The dual-purpose, on/off road, trail bike is enormously popular in Italy, and growing of course elsewhere – at least, for street only use! Italy has long produced 'street scramblers'. This 750 Pantah engined Cagiva shown at Milan in 1983 was naturally enough called the *Elefant*; it is after the style of Moto Morini's Camel and Kangaroo, plus the Japanese large capacity off-roaders. The Pantah engine has a proven record in the desert, too (Rothman's Pyramid Rally, Egypt, 1983)

Right Flash exposure of a Ducati Pantah TT2 in early 1984. This one is special – it's a Sports Motor Cycles Racing, Steve Wynne-built Harris-framed road racer equipped for road use, with Cagiva on the tank. Note the instruments which hide a headlamp, the Shaw filler on the tank and the Reynolds tubing label on the frame. Even with the standard 600 engine some might argue that it would see off anything cross-country – except a KB2 Bimota?
The Laverda triple engine in the background also sits in a Harris frame

4 Bologna — *Taglioni's desmodromics* — Ducati

Above Some people love their Ducati to the extent that they name a couple of clothes shops that way. Location – Chiswick, West London. Car – Lancia HPE 2000 IE

Right Little single cylinder Ducatis are hard to date and define: this one appears to be a 450 Mark III of 1968. Rest assured it was one imported into the USA by Berliner of New Jersey during the heyday of Ducati sales in that country and has been lovingly kept ever since. Shot here at the Rock Store one Sunday in May 1982; it was amongst strange company

Above The very last of the factory Ducati singles were like this 450 Desmo shot at Woods Motor Shop in Glendale, California. It's a 1974 version with the Tartarini styling (boss of Italjet) and some non-stock parts such as the dog leg levers, Dunstall exhaust and K&N air filter. Check out the lack of decals too. Still, very fine

Right Every Ducati enthusiast worth his salt knows about their bevel drive valve gear – whether pure Taglioni-style desmo controlled or just plain 'ordinary'. Each cylinder head is assembled by hand one at a time, mostly by women. None get fitted to a barrel, and into a bike, until all is well

Don't know what this is, exactly, but it's worth showing. The engine is a 'round' case 750 vee-twin in a special German-built (?) frame with many 750 cycle parts too. It's a curious mixture of old and new parts and styles. The exhaust shape is very-Magni MV and the wheelbase looks very long — even longer, perhaps, than the already long factory frame. However, all this is to be expected from bikes to be seen on the front at Douglas during TT week, in the Isle of Man. Especially those from West Germany

Above Seen also on the Isle of Man in June 1982 was this near stock 750SS. The rear carrier is ingenious and doesn't alter the bike itself but the colour isn't right even though it's glamorous. Perhaps the best balanced Italian sports roadster ever, or has one to argue in favour of Laverda's 750SFC? Whatever, there's no arguing that the early 1970s produced a zenith in this style of bike

Left 'Why doesn't anyone want me?' Unloved of Minneapolis. The 860GT Ducati vee-twin is not appreciated by many enthusiasts for its styling and tame engine. The severe square design came from the drawing board of Giorgetto Giugiaro, founder of Ital Design, with a car design reputation second to none. It flopped. This nearly original example, even down to the colour and exhausts, survives in Minnesota in 1983

Above and left 900SS – essentially the same bike with two different tank insignia. The word 'Ducati' featured here was designed by Giugiaro and is a classic piece of type design. The 900SS is a late type (1981?) with Conti silencers and Speedline wheels, and dual seat and is somewhat diluted from the original spec. in terms of speed but slightly 'comfortised' instead. Note the 'square' crankcase sides. Shot at the Vee-Twin Rally in Shaftesbury in Dorset, in 1982.
The tank on the left is a factory item, the one on the bike appears to be a substitute

Above A tired looking Ford Transit van sits in Oxford with this Ducati 900SS reproduction on one side and a Moto Guzzi Le Mans on the other. Nice work. The van is run by Oxford Motorcycle Engineers who work out of a small shop which oozes Italian motorcycles of most kinds. The spec. of the air brushed sports roadster is around 1981, again with dual seat, Speedline wheels and Contis – no winkers

Right Here's another German registered 900SS in the Isle of Man. This one comes with wire spoke wheels, a Darmah style half-fairing and yet a later dual seat with locking cubby hole. Those lovely Conti pipes help set-off the whole custom work. Nice

All and overleaf The MHR or Hailwood Rep or 900SS Mike Hailwood Replica was a spark of marketing genius unparalleled by Ducati Meccanica before or since. The late, great Mike the Bike wins in the TT in 1978 on a non-factory bike and the factory produces an anything but true replica. Its sales have been enormous and it's an excellent motorcycle. These pages feature a late two-piece fairing and steel fuel tank. Overleaf is a replica replica (?) with half-fairing

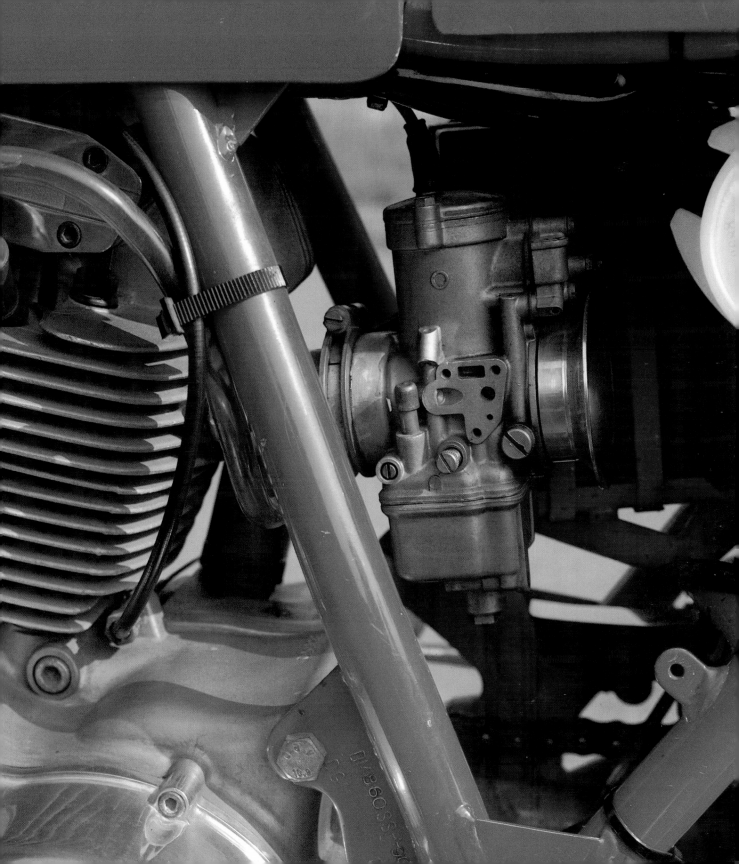

The Vee-Twin Rally held each year at Shaftesbury in Dorset is really an excuse for certain Italian motorcycle enthusiasts to get together and then hurl themselves around the English countryside both safely and quickly. Ducati, Guzzi and Morini riders abound whilst Harley-Davidson, Vincent and Honda riders tend to stay away. If it's sunny then a fun weekend is had by all.

This happy rider is aboard a Ducati Darmah, which one exactly can't be told from the photograph because the paint is special, as is the exhaust, but the drilled discs, the seat and fairing suggest a 900SSD. And that essentially means desmo heads and electric starting with I + I seating. This Darmah got close to the performance of the 900SS. Such is the capacity of accessory manufacturers in copying factory parts, even creating replica parts themselves, and such is the suitability of big Ducati vee-twins for 'parts swopping', it is becoming increasingly difficult to tell one model from another. Change the fairing and seat and one model becomes another!

Behind is a 3½ Morini Sport on the left

Back to the Rock Store on Mulholland Highway up
in canyon country north of the San Fernando
Valley in Southern California. It's the heaven sent
meeting place for Sunday bikers – all types feel
happy there including this 500 Pantah in
immaculate state. Admirers of all ages drink cola
or beer (in brown paper bags) and enjoy the
atmosphere. Lovely early example

Left and below The 600 Pantah used a restyled fairing and seat first tried on very late 500s. It received a beefed up clutch and gearbox too, and not before time. Many people were waiting for the 'promised 750' version but that now has to come from Cagiva. Nevertheless, the 600 'real' Pantah is there to remind us of how a middle weight can scratch the Japanese finesse. This perfect sample was found in Glendale, California complete with single seat hump installed.

The two frames exhibited at Milan are both those for a Pantah engine. The top one is the factory racing monoshock frame which needs the engine to fill the centre whilst the one below is the standard road bike frame but painted red (probably for Cagiva?). The road and race bike fairings and seats hid the special shape that make both a pair of the finest handling motorcycles ever made.

Verlicchi SpA make frames for many Italian bike manufacturers and are an example of the massive industrial sub-strata available to them

Overleaf The 1984 version of the Ducati 900S2 complete with all red bodywork and frame, and new belly pan. Compare this shape with that of the 1983 S2 on the back cover of this book. It's a fine looking (maybe even our last look) sports motorcycle fit for the era. Note the new engine cases which are readied for the new Mille or 1000 engine. This actual machine is still 860 cc

55

5 Mandello del Lario — *Carcano's heritage* — Guzzi

Both below Justifiable pride accompanies the Guzzi eagle wherever it appears. The show stand insignia towered above the Guzzi stand at the 1983 Milan show. The bird can turn either way! The sweater is a replica of the factory team 'shirts' worn by riders in the nineteen twenties in the days when jodpurs and calf-length lace-up leather boots were *de rigueur*

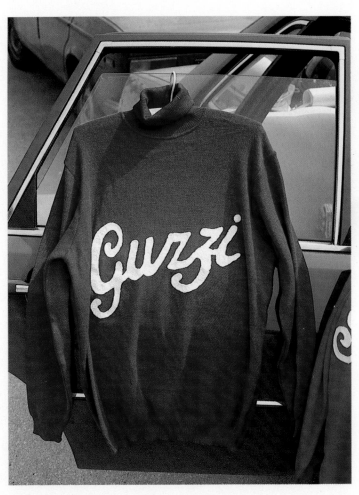

Overleaf Late model Guzzi Falcone on show in Bassano del Grappa, near Vicenza in Italy, one Sunday morning. Local club offered lots to see. Owner is the man in the peaked cap

Above and left Moto Guzzi in America has a long and pretty fruitful history. The tank is an early, big vee-twin spare part for sale at Hershey in Pennsylvania in October 1982. Florida family dealership had held it since new – carefully greased to avoid rust.

Not everyone rode to Sturgis, South Dakota in 1983 on a Harley-Davidson. This 'angel' went by 850 Guzzi Eldorado even if it was equipped with footboards, high handlebars (ape hangers?) and aftermarket exhausts. Come to think of it, it's not so strange, for Guzzi aggressively went for H-D in the market place with the Eldorado and later California models in the 1970s. Some police departments even threw out their home-brewed Harleys for Guzzis

Back to the Vee-Twin Rally in Shaftesbury for this British spec. Guzzi 850 T3 California. The screen and white/black seat are right for the bike and the panniers are Krauser-like add ons. With shaft drive and the T3 engine in a nice, lazy state of tune (note square bore Dell'Orto carburettors), there's no better traditional touring motorcycle. If needs be, though, it can handle with the best of them because underneath are Guzzi's familiar frame and cycle parts

This is the latest Guzzi California, known as the 'II' and produced in 1983, again at the same Vee-Twin Rally. Note the strong change in emphasis with this model away from the strictly functional tourer to the Harley-Davidson clone. Note the tail lamp, extended Harleyesque buddy seat and rail, deeply valanced mudguards and the white paint. More show than go with this one . . . although underneath it still is real Guzzi motorcycle

Below and right The Moto Guzzi V7 Sport is a stunning motorcycle of the very early nineteen-seventies, preceding the disc braked 750s and 850 Le Mans. Both were photographed in mid 1982 when each was at least ten years old; the red one in Shaftesbury, Dorset, England; the green one at Misano, south of Rimini in Italy.

These drum braked sports roadsters are highly prized today, and rightly so. Part of their charm is their simple looks, handbuilt feel and nice touches, such as the height adjustable handlebars. The green one has a facsimile Bill Lomas signature painted on the tank . . .

Below and right The Le Mans (subsequently to be called the Mark I, after the announcement of the Mark II) took the marketplace by storm with its unsubtle looks. Here was an outwardly aggressive café racer, or as some Americans would call it, a 'flash bike', which could deliver speed, handling and reliability. Neither of the two shots here show the 'dayglo orange' surrounding colour of the headlamp. . . .

The Le Mans was timed right, priced right and sold right! Thousands have been sold since 1973/74. The bike below is an English spec. version with the flatter dual seat, while the other is an Italian version with the 'humped' dual seat. Long, low and remarkably fast, even for a relatively unsophisticated push rod engined, shaft drive bike

Above Guzzi Le Mans in the Californian sunshine. The round barrels of these earlier bikes are preferred by many and no one can be anything other than impressed by that large bore Dell'Orto pumper carburettor

Right Mark II Le Mans with minor customizing at the Rock Store, north of Los Angeles. Obviously a proud man in a sea of universal Japanese motorcycles (UJMs), something a Le Mans stays well away from

Left Le Mans Mark III in Osceola, Wisconsin (to US spec.). Absolutely stock except for the bar end mirror and lack of dayglo orange fairing stripes. In 1984 it's still one of the best looking and satisfying bikes to ride. Period

Overleaf Two nonplussed Italian 'road' Police on their Guzzi V50s in Bassano del Grappa in the Dolomite foothills. Red mark on the fuel tank is dye from the officer's trouser stripes. They always get their man

Below Clever touch to make you buy. White faced, centrally mounted rev counter and smaller, offset speedo. The rider of this Le Mans Mark III is looking for a European speedo which reads past 80 mph

Above The 'little' vee-twin Guzzis now come in a multitude of guises from 350 through to 650, with 750 looming. This is the 650 semi-tourer, or V65 SP, photographed in the Champs-Elysées in Paris in late 1983. Man with stick was flattered

Left Fashion takes over. Rectangular headlamps have come in with a rush and seem here to stay. They are no more powerful than round ones and not normally legal in North America, where this V50 Monza was photographed. It must be allowed because the quantity of such machines sold is below the terms of the regulation

Guzzi has found great sales strength under its ownership by de Tomaso. Bikes have moved off the dealer's showroom floor and the money has enabled some interesting development work to take place. This V35 Imola II is the latest (as of the Milan show in November 1983) 350 sports roadster and comes with four-valve heads (and 16 inch wheels) as its most important technical innovation, and the most stunning looks

At the same Milan show the Monza II came in
white to balance the red of the V35. With the
eagle back on the tank and clever use of fashion
and function (re belly pan and seat/tank fixing)
these little sportsters should have a good future
ahead of them. Time will tell

6 Breganze — *for racing the Dolomite foothills* — Laverda

Below There was life at Moto Laverda before the big twins and triples. This little 100 Sport of about 1956 is a gem of sports bike with its lively push-rod engine and sparkling handling. Quite one of the most stylish lightweights of its day, too. This correctly restored model lives in Milan

Below Sadly Laverda's early 1960's 200 twin wasn't and isn't as well respected although it's still a worthy machine. This one was offered at the world's biggest automotive flea market at Hershey in 1982. The $300 Laverda buys a better machine than the $450 for the 'Austin' Nash Metropolitan behind

Overleaf If you are a police chief in Italy, and you are lucky, then you go by Laverda 750GTL. Caught in Bassano del Grappa, just up the road from Breganze where the bike was made, the man is smiling and rightly so. These big parallel twins offer comfort with impressive command

81

Left and below Around 19,000 Laverda 750 twins
were made in an eight year period between 1968
and 1976 in numerous guises. In their day they had
an excellent reputation for speed, handling and
reliability. They performed as police bikes and
endurance racers, all with success. Here are two
shots taken at the Ballacraine Hotel meeting of the
International Laverda Owners Club during TT
week on the Isle of Man in 1982. The green 750 is
a 1974 SF2 whilst the two orange bikes either side
of it are SFCs, either of 1974 or 1975

Above Italian registered Laverda 1000 triples outside Italy are a rare sight; they are fairly rare in Italy too. This is a black framed (1978?) cast wheel 3CL in Douglas in the Isle of Man. It has a factory (?) three-into-one exhaust, non-standard rear shockabsorbers and a home-made rear carrier and drilled discs. No mistaking what it is

Left Shooting the breeze. Sunday riding, two up with matching leathers, is done by many throughout Italy. This couple, note her high fashion sleeveless 'puffa', are aboard a Laverda 1000 triple with seat unit by Cico, guru of Vicenza. Their Dainese leathers are made close by, as is the bike itself

Above An over painted 180 Jota of 1981 shot in Garden Grove, California. Note the illegal Jota pipes from England. Not a bike for a 55 mph speed limit

Right For 1982 Moto Laverda altered the crankshaft throw arrangement from 180 to 120 degrees and transformed the bike. Very, very fast, no question

A British special using a late type 180 Jota 1000 engine. This is the Motodd monoshock in early 1983 taken at Donington Park race circuit. Lots of money has been spent in addition to that needed for the special frame: Dymag three-spoke wheels don't come cheap. Is it possible to improve on Italian styling, always?

Another British special but using Italian style bodywork. This Formula Mirage comes from the Slater brothers and uses Italian Motoplast-inspired seat/tank unit and Astralite composite wheels. A second Formula sits behind the 1200, it's a 120 Jota with its standard fairing colour coded in. Both go fast

Overleaf A multitude of Laverda triples shot at Three Cross Motorcycles in early 1984. The winter sun has already melted the snow flurries. From left to right: 1984 (RGA) Jota with English built fairing, 1983 RGA, 1982 RGS, 1979 Jota Cropredy Liberator and 1978/79 standard factory Jota

Above and left 1982 Laverda 500 Montjuich. This is an English specification version of the 500 twin with the second series bodywork inspired by Motoplast. This fairing was frame mounted and it too was manufactured in England as was the original bikini handlebar mounted fairing and seat of the first series bike.

The Montjuich (Catalan spelling omits the 'h') is a highly tuned ex-Alpino/Zeta roadster named after the 24 hour Barcelona endurance racing class winning bike of 1978.

A 'real' Laverda after the spirit of the 750SFC and later Jota

Below and right No book on Italian motorcycles can be anything near complete without a photograph of Laverda's 1000 V6 endurance racer. No one who has heard the engine run can be anything other than mesmerised by its sweetness and apparent power. Although it ran under race conditions only once, at the Bol d'Or in 1979, it lacked little that would have not have enabled it to win sooner or later.

In short it's a magnificent piece of engineering that was both bold and interesting. Its career failed because of a lack of money . . .

Above and left Laverda's 1000 RGS was a masterstroke. After nearly eight years of production the factory revamped the triple package to look like this – superb. Underneath things were much different. Left, early production bike at the factory; above, US spec. in Glendale

Left The powerhouse at Moto Laverda. On the right is Massimo Laverda, managing director brother of Piero; in the check jacket is ex MV designer Bocchi concerned in 1984 with the design of the new generation of Laverdas. Man in the blue coat is chief draughtsman and the test rider, aboard a prototype RGS, is about to circle the factory test track where the photographer is standing. The sunshine helps

Above For 1984 Moto Laverda announced yet another marque racing series in Italy for 'young riders'. The bike they all have to ride is the new 125LB first shown at the 1983 Milan show. Behind are potential customers of this delightful lightweight roadster equipped here with the 'race kit'. Lots of fun

7 Bologna — *the other side of town* — Morini

Above Moto Morini is another family firm producing interesting roadsters, at least for export. This is their 3½ (350 cc) Strada of about 1977 vintage with drum front brake. These bikes are renowned for their supreme handling and smoothness

Right A later disc braked Strada shot in New York's twilight from a taxi cab window. Not a common sight in the land of the pot hole

This happy Italian has just ridden his 3½ Sport to Paris and parked it under the Eifel Tower. Apart from the hole in the silencer it's a well-equipped machine for fast road riding – what it lacks in the way of straightline speed it well makes up around corners and across country

The Morini 350 is a popular machine in that most popular capacity for Italian riders. This is a 1982 spec. Sport with red and black paint in profusion and cast wheels. Although not generally successful on the race track these middleweight machines make ideal roadsters. Shot here in northern Italy one Sunday in April

Above The bare essentials. An English spec.
Morini's instrument panel of 1982/83 vintage

Right A remarkably large number of accessories
exist for the small Morini range. This bike shows
off special fairing, seat and exhaust to make it a
handsome looking special. Shaftesbury 1982

Above and left The 500 Maestro (in the UK) vee-twin everyone hoped would be very fast, something the 350 isn't really. However, it didn't come up to expectation for most people although it does provide enough power for two up riding in comfort. It's still the same well balanced roadster the 350 is with just a little more guts. Doesn't rev quite so freely.
Italian graphics still win awards though

Above Both the Laverda 1000 RGS and this Morini 500 Turbo were styled by the RG Studio in Rome and both were shown simultaneously at the Milan show in 1981. The RGS made it into the showroom, the Morini Turbo hasn't seen the light of day yet. More's the pity

Left This handsome Morini 500 Sport was photographed in Costa Mesa, California outside then Laverda specialist Rickey Racer's shop. After the Japanese invasion it's a delight to see

Morini scored well with this off-road version of the 500, the Camel. Like its 350 brother, the Kangaroo, it's a strong alternative in the enduro market for the other European and Japanese manufacturers who tend to rule the roost with two-strokes. Bike bore four-strokes in this configuration are proving more competitive than ever before – the bike's good on road too

At the 1983 Milan show Morini offered this K2
version of the familiar 350/500 Sport. It shows a
change in direction in their styling, and one which
doesn't follow anything from the 500 Turbo either.
Italian design used to offer mostly simplicity and
the 'stripped' look. Now, it's changing towards
streamlining and covering up. Who's copying
whom?

8 Verghera — *nothing but fire engine red* — MV Agusta

The classic road racing MV four is perhaps the
most charismatic Italian motorcycle ever made.
Here is Nello Pagani 'parading' the factory's 500 cc
four cylinder at the Misano historic motorcycle
meeting in 1982. Rare sight and rare sound –
ripping silk?
Fortunately the MV Agusta factory still have a few
of their racers ready for 'classic' events

Above and right Number I again. It's not for nothing that MVs are often described as painted in 'fire engine red'. What price a factory MV? In the background are a couple of works Mondials and a Guzzi Le Mans Mark I

Overleaf Maurice Ogier's MV leathers are an artform in themselves. He's aboard the ex-Hannah Paton 500 twin GP bike at Misano in 1982

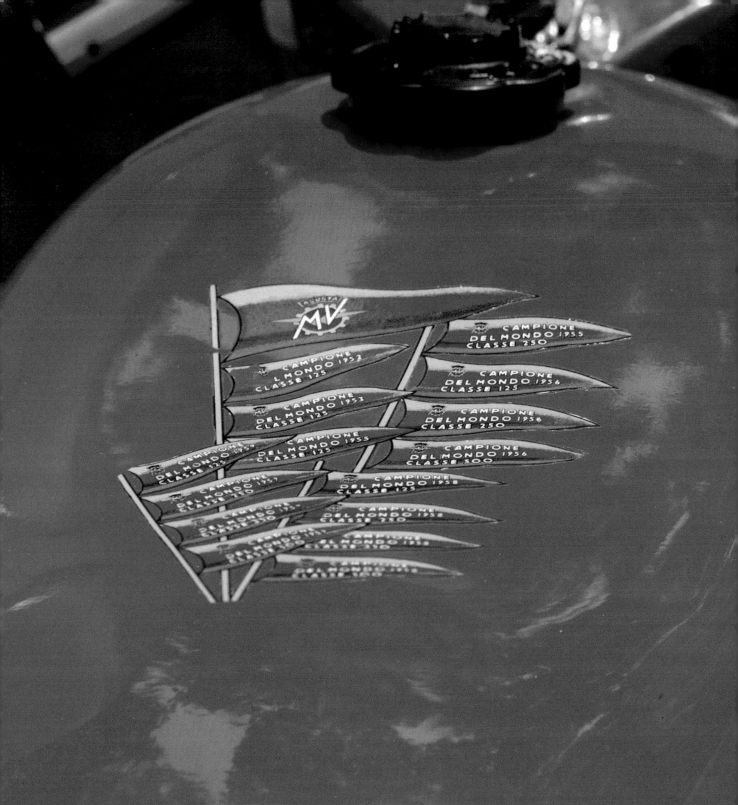

Left Thirty-seven constructor's and 38 rider's world championships went to MV Agusta since the Second War. Here's a typical tank transfer used by them in the late 1950s, post 1958, on some of their production bikes

Below A German registered MV Agusta four. Expert opinion suggests that this is a converted 750 with America tank, Magni side panels, right hand gear shift and a strange four-into-one exhaust. What is it?

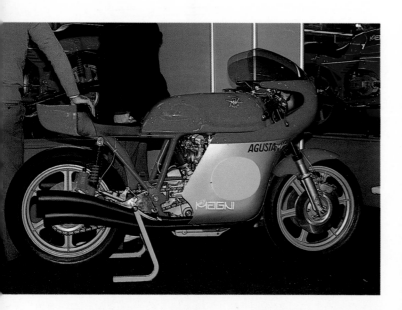

Above Arturo Magni showed this 750 four with GP type tank at the Milan show in 1983 some five years or more since the factory stopped production completely. This road-racing styled road bike features his chain drive conversion and exhaust, and his son's EPM wheels. Yellow number disc suggests a 500, but certainly a 750

Right MV Agusta ready for the *Classic Bike* sponsored 'parade' at the 1982 TT. Lots of Magni parts on Bill Curgenven's 861 replica of the 1972 Imola F750 bike

9 More colour on the map

Above Since the demise of MV as both a racing concern and a motorcycle manufacturing company Arturo Magni has been preparing both MV specials and supplying parts, and designing this type of machine. It's his special frame for the BMW horizontal twin – or put another way – the marrying of German engine with Italian cycle parts

Left Sunday morning motorcycling in Italy. Full leathers, both Japanese and Italian sports bikes and 50 miles to a second breakfast, fast

Right Remember Ducati's bolt-on engine which powered the first Cucciolos in 1946 or so? Back in 1983 the pedal-cycle-motor-cycle was back again with a vengeance. Tiffany from Italjet, no matter how loose the skirt

Below Italy produces a large number of components to build motorcycles with. Here's one of Segale's road racing bikes ready for the 1984 endurance racing season. It's Suzuki 750 four powered and like Bimota beautifully made. Their trademark of the drilled rear engine mounting is just visible to be balanced with design on the rear seat bump . . .

Overleaf Tasty Gilera Saturno 500 special ready to compete in one of Italy's 'regularity runs' at Misano. These runs are a cross between a parade and a race – safer and perhaps more fun. . . . Swiss Samuele Beltrami's tuned road engine sits in a special 1960s-type frame, Ceriani forks and 4LS Fontana front brake; it's modelled on Paulo Campanello's Italian Championship and GP bike of the 1960s

TIFFANY

From ITALY With Love